Praise for *Animals Out-There W-i-l-d: A Bestiary in English and ASL Gloss*

The poems in this stunning collection are both playful and provocative, vulnerable and intimate. Via delicious imagery, Luczak maintains a primal curiosity and gentleness of spirit despite his heart-wrenching awareness of human ignorance and cruelty. His reverence for the natural world is palpable. In the book's closing poem "Wild Animals, Again," the poet prophesizes, "animals will outlive us when we find ourselves unable to speak the language of connection." This gorgeous collection is a testament to the power of poetry, transcending barriers and fostering understanding between worlds. I will return to Luczak's poems again and again with a sense of wonderment.

Ellen Lord, author of *Relative Sanity: Poems*

In one of many astute insights into the creature world in this magnificent book, Raymond Luczak tells us that animals' stories "about us are their most powerful tool for survival." But these poems are also reminders that stories about them can help save us. Luczak give us two distinct languages — a beautifully attentive written English and a dynamic, inventive American Sign Language gloss. His added genius, though, is to evoke vastly more — the individual languages of any signer's specific hands and face and body, of course, as well as the infinite languages of creation, through which every living being, including each of us, contributes to nature's conversation.

Jonathan Johnson, author of *May Is an Island*

Animals Out-There W-i-l-d: A Bestiary in English and ASL Gloss is a magical book that works its spells in musical silence. The work recalls Beethoven's *The Creatures of Prometheus*. The book is more than a *pas de deux* between Art and Life, but a beautiful ballet between the creative properties of related languages. Luczak endows the creatures of his bestiary — from tardigrade to bear to dancing firefly — with a new life in the reader's imagination: where ASL gesture and English speech combine in vital new forms, both familiar and strange.

Eric Thomas Norris, author of *That Time I Met Einstein and Other Catastrophes*

Raymond Luczak's *Animals Out-There W-i-l-d: A Bestiary in English and ASL Gloss* is a feat of leaping language, a delightful and surprising conversation between English and the American Sign Language gloss that Luczak has created in performing his own poetry. These poems invite us to inhabit their bodies and to examine all the contours of possibility within each line (as well as its counterpart), to attend to noticing the more-than-human world, "a choir that has / nothing to do with us / humans."

Ching-In Chen, author of *recombinant*

Far from Atlantis

Chlorophyll

Lunafly

once upon a twin

Bokeh Focus

A Babble of Objects

The Kiss of Walt Whitman Still on My Lips

How to Kill Poetry

Road Work Ahead

Mute

This Way to the Acorns

St. Michael's Fall

Animals Out-There W-i-l-d

A BESTIARY IN ENGLISH AND ASL GLOSS

Animals Out-There W-i-l-d Raymond Luczak

A BESTIARY IN
ENGLISH AND ASL GLOSS

UNBOUND EDITION PRESS

Atlanta

FIRST EDITION

Printed in the United States of America

LIBRARY OF CONGRESS RECORD

Name: Luczak, Raymond, 1965 — author.
Title: Animals Out-There W-i-l-d: A Bestiary in English and ASL Gloss / Raymond Luczak.
Edition: First edition.
Published: Atlanta : Unbound Edition Press, 2024.

LCCN: 2024937417
LCCN Permalink: https://lccn.loc.gov/2024937417
ISBN: 979-8-9892333-9-7 (fine softcover)

Designed by Eleanor Safe and Joseph Floresca
Printed by Bookmobile, Minneapolis, MN
Distributed by Itasca Books

123456789

Unbound Edition Press
1270 Caroline Street, Suite D120
Box 448
Atlanta, GA 30307

*The Unbound Edition Press logo and name are
registered trademarks of Unbound Edition LLC.*

PERMANENT

for Margaret Arnold

Contents

Animals Out-There
W-i-l-d
A BESTIARY IN
ENGLISH AND ASL GLOSS

Notes

On ASL Gloss

American Sign Language (ASL) gloss is simply using English words and ASL idioms in the ASL sign order. Just to be clear: There is no standardized ASL gloss system at all. It is impossible to convey even a fraction of all the rich nuances of an ASL sentence on paper. For instance, how does one show facial expressions (i.e., emotional inflections), the location for each person (or animal) referenced in the signing space, the spatial relationships between these people, the sign dialects, and so on? In this book, however, I occasionally use regular [brackets] to indicate generic handshapes, and place classifiers in {curly brackets}. (According to the "Classifier constructions in sign language" article on Wikipedia, "classifiers differ from signs in their morphology: signs consist of a single morpheme [the smallest meaningful unit in a language]. Signs are composed of three meaningless phonological features: handshape, location, and movement. A classifier, on the other hand, can consist of many morphemes. Specifically, the handshape, location, and movement are all meaningful on their own.") Words set in SMALL CAPS usually refer to lip movements (particularly when prefixed with the phrase LIPS:) or facial inflections. These poems in ASL gloss are meant to be read silently and visualized.

On the Word "Yooper"

The *New Oxford American Dictionary* defines the word "Yooper" as "a native or inhabitant of the Upper Peninsula of Michigan." The word was derived from the acronym U.P. plus the person-ending "er," rather like how "write" + "er" became "writer." The word "Yooper" was apparently coined during the 1970s. I'd always said that I came from *above* the mitten half of Michigan, but when I started to see the word used more frequently, I began to identify myself as a "da Yooper."

My Yooper identity never relied on jokes about the not-so-lightbulb-bright Finns known as Aino and Toivo or speaking "Yoopanese." Half of my childhood was spent in the Houghton-Hancock area, where the largest concentration of Finns outside of Finland existed, but as a deaf boy, I was only there to learn how to speak. I couldn't simply overhear the jokes or absorb the Yooper way of talking, which is apparently heavily influenced by the Finns who had emigrated to the U.P. in the 19th century. I don't think I have a Yooper dialect; just a flat nasal voice. Aside from skating badly at ice rinks and tobogganing superbly down Copper Peak, I never engaged in winter sports. My family was too poor to own a snowmobile or afford a set of skis, let alone score a day pass at one of the six local ski resorts. But we kids had the woods and the cave-ins across the street, where we explored no matter the season, and Lake Superior was a twenty-minute drive away. For this book, I've chosen to focus on the wild animals found in the Upper Peninsula.

I.

Wild Animals Out There

Take these, my hands.

Skin: the coat for all seasons.

Bones: the foundation for the house of me.

Nerves: the telephone wires to the brain.

Veins: the many rivers to the heart.

*

look hands-mine {these}

dress same no-matter happen-happen skin that

body mine same-same house bones what foundation

n-e-r-v-e-s similar-similar {phone-call-both-sides} connect
    brain {mind-explode LIPS: POW}

heart {veins-spread-all-over-body back-to-heart}

Do not speak.

Finger to the lips.

A voice
is noise.

Watch these—my hands—and ask nothing.
Eloquence will come to you soon enough.

*

speak finish-finish-finish

{finger-to-the-lips}

voice what
noise-bang-noise-bang

watch-me sign-sign you-confuse worry not
visualize mind-pop-up soon will

Aristotle had said the failure to speak
was also the failure of intelligence.

What a colossal failure of imagination!

And the price that Deaf people have
had to pay over centuries!

*

a-r-i-s-t-o-t-l-e {NAME-SIGN Aristotle} believe
person speak can't mean person smart not

Aristotle smart not
proof have

hearing people believe Aristotle right
look-down deaf people comparable animals
since-then centuries

Sit.

Close your ears.

Wait.

Silence is not what you think it is.

It is the eye-sound of no motion.
No flicker of light,
no sigh of curtain flapping from the wind.

The world is a sheet of glass amplified
in the periphery of my eyes.

Yet I am no animal.

*

sit-right-there

{cover-ears}

wait-wait patient-patient

hearing-people think silence equal sound none

silence what
motion anywhere none
window curtain {wind-move-move} none

me {eyeballs-gaze-left-right}
world open-out-there glass {circular}

me animal ?? of-course not

Long before 1760, when
Abbe Charles-Michel de lÉpée founded
the first public school for the Deaf
(the Institut National de Jeunes Sourdes de Paris),
Deaf people were seen as animals in human form.

When they finally connected with each other, usually by
    accident,
their hands sparked lightning and thundered away the weight
    of years
yoked by their hearing families who had treated them like
    horses.

Hearing people were always struck dumb
by the unexpected vision of barbarians lighting up brighter
    than any sun.
These weren't just gestures.

Inside each Deaf person is an oracle,
waiting to unleash language from the gods
who've already tired of hearing voices babble.

*

all-along history before 17-60

a-b-b-e c-h-a-r-l-e-s-m-i-c-h-e-l d-e l-é-p-é-e set-up first deaf
   school

i-n-s-t-i-t-u-t national d-e j-e-u-n-e-s s-o-u-r-d-e-s d-e paris

hearing look-down deaf people same-same animals happen
   look human

if deaf lucky hit meet-each-other

figure-out quickly communicate how

sign-create-sign

all-those-years hearing family oppress-them

{weight-off-their-shoulders}

hearing always gawk {jaw-drop} watch

think deaf animal {mind-shock}

sign-sign wow-wow

not gesture clear sign-sign

deaf inside power have

god-god-god give-give-give-deaf

language champ push-away

hearing annoy-annoy babble-babble-in-ear

Animals.

They carry a lot of secrets.
To the untrained human eye, they look
identical to each other
but they smell very different to each other.

They carbon-copy everything about us
in a flash of telepathy to their own kind.
This is how they endure.

Stories about us are their most powerful tool for survival.

*

animals have what

secrets
human {look-across} animals {look-same-across}
animals look same but {each-across} smell-smell different-
    different-across

animals {telepathy-across} their-children
explain them confront-us how

stories theirs-across survive how that

Sit.

The woods up north are full of rustle.
It isn't just the winds that quicksilver everywhere.

Breathe.

In the heart encircled by trees,
a hundred pairs of eyes of all kinds
are watching you.

Do not move.

They know from how you've entered their space,
you are a barbarian.

The smartphone in your hand
is a warning to all who scent you.
It means you do not belong.

You don't know their language.
You've already failed them.

sit-there

woods north out-there {wind-leaves-rustle}
winds {move-through} that-all {shake-head-no}

b-r-e-a-t-h-e breathe-breathe

{circle-tree-around} center
eyes different-different {up-all-over-left up-all-over-right}
{all-watch-you}

stay-still move not

{all-watch-you} know you-enter wood {big-head-ego}
you b-a-r-b-a-r-i-a-n

phone {point-to-curved-hand}
warn-warn {all-watch-you}
you fit-in woods not
why

language {theirs-theirs-theirs}
you not-know you fail finish

A Yooper Bestiary

Tardigrade | t-a-r-d-i-g-r-a-d-e

eight-legged
they slow-step
a steady march
among moss
and lichen
a fallen log
is an entire planet
cratered by
the meteor
showers of season
anyplace beyond
this log
is unfathomable
like the Upper Peninsula

{four-hands-atop-each-other-crawl-slow} where
m-o-s-s
l-i-c-h-e-n
tree {fall-down-bounce-settle}
same-same p-l-a-n-e-t
weather {year-round}
rain-rain {straight-down}
snow {drift-down}
{influence-fallen-tree}
{four-hands-atop-each-other-crawl}
envision world big beyond {fallen-log}
impossible
{out-there} M-i-c-h {handshape-map point-top}
U-p-p-e-r P-e-n-i-n-s-u-l-a

Owl | owl

never could find them
perched among the gray
pine trees turning old
from not enough water
they'd been planted
too close together
their fingers locked
in thirst for water
rivuletting underground
but the owls knew exactly
where to hide
in the forest of my dreaming
cause how else
could they know so much

tree-tree-tree   old   p-i-n-e   gray   why   thirst   water

{down}   enough-enough   {head-shake-no}   tree-tree-tree

long-ago   land   {all-over}   empty-all-over

sow-sow-tight-together   trees-grow   {fingers-mangle-stuck}

compete-tight   thirst   water   {down}

but   o-w-l-s   {up-there}   chin-pow   know   exact   where

hide   overlook   tree-tree-tree   while   me-dream-dream

lost   wander-wander   {up-there}

them-watch-me   {NODS}   genius-knowledge

Deer | deer

whenever I saw them
they never had antlers
but this one
the way he held his head
badge of honor
not even twenty feet away
his eyes lasered
into me like he knew
far more than I'd ever know
those antlers both
a repository and reliquary
jeweled with stories
long ago and now us
I felt antlerless to gaze back

all-along see-see deer always female
antler-antler none but one {point-to} antlers have
head {neck-hold-strong LIPS: FIRM}
prove himself finish
him far {head-shake-no} close wow
eyes-turn-eyes stare-me
{eyes-staring-diving-into-me}
himself {chin-jaded} genius-knowledge
me nothing
antlers have inside library
r-e-l-i-c-s story-story many
long-ago
now us ?? destroy them
me antlers-drop-embarrass {look-back}

Eagle | eagle

found with a broken wing
she was brought to the zoo
her world is a window
no more sky and treetops
just reliable meals
she stands bitterly
on a fallen log
punctuated by talons
her proximity discomforting me
she narrows her eyes
at me daring to take pictures
the only way she can survive
is her endless calculating
the thrill of kill

herself w-i-n-g {shoulder-dislocate} fly can't
someone find bring z-o-o
now l-o-g {rest-ground talons-grip STARE}
world watch-her window
s-k-y {stretched-hand rise-up-through}
trees {tree-tops-far-distance} fly can't
now window herself {pow-close-up}
eyes stare-me {BITTER}
me take-pictures dangerous
herself survive how
{talons-grip} thoughts-flutter-flutter
steady-steady {STARE}
kill me how

Raccoon | raccoon

nights they spread out
in their Mardi Gras finery
masks and striped tails
nobody would think
the world is a feast
but they know where
to knock over trash cans
ah the joy of spilled beans
and rotting tomatoes
and stinky fish sticks
after each binge
they belly-whoop it
up the electrical poles

every-night raccoon many dress-up-fancy
same-same m-a-r-d-i g-r-a-s
mask black {glasses-tight-around-face}
t-a-i-l tail r-i-n-g gray black alternate-alternate
people general believe food free world not
but raccoon chin-pow feet {push} garbage cans
{fall-over} l-i-d {fall-off} people food not-want
{spill-all-over} b-e-a-n-s {first-item-list}
tomatoes b-r-u-i-s-e disgusting
fish s-t-i-c-k-s not finish eat smell-smell awful
raccoon eat-eat-eat {pats-belly} finish
electric {pole raccoon-belly-waddle-up tongue-out}
sneak-off dark
home again satisfied sleep

Bedbug | bed bug

on the coldest of days
my soul tastes like chicken
not much meat either
the grass is brown
everything thirsty
hungry for bone
vials of blood
seasoned with prey
every night I step inside
they mottle in shadows
salivating to cherry-pick
my scalp on the pillow
suddenly stitched with itches
I am roast

today winter true-biz freeze cold

        me-feel inside what

            my soul same-same chicken

thin meat thumb-little

        grass out-there brown

           world thirst-thirst more-more

crave bone crave blood

        every-night

           me-enter home

little-bugs {DISGUST} hide dark

        wait-wait

           me-leap-bed

{little-bugs-rise-up-shoulder-head}

        itch-itch-here itch-itch-there

           {LIPS: FINISH} finish

Horse | horse

they must've galloped
all over my bed
cause when I woke up
I found hoofprints
all over my bedsheets
I rolled over them
flattening the grassy creases
remembering the peat
clinging to the posts
trying to fence
in untamed dreams
whinnying against
bitter winds

me-wake-up confused why
seem bed {around-me} h-o-o-f-p-r-i-n-t-s
bed sheets {crumple} grass
me-roll-over flat
me-mind pop-up vague-vague
fence {four-posts}
dirt {cling-post}
why-why
dream-dream mine same-same
horses {gallop-gallop-every-which-way}
angry gallop-gallop anywhere can't
wind-wind strong
horses bitter

Opossum | opossum

late at night
she gripped
a bottom branch
of the aspen
she didn't move
for a moment
maybe she thought
she'd blend right
into the tree and fool me
I didn't move either
death breathed
momentarily between us
before her long snout
finally twitched

happen one night me walking
spot-notice
o-p-o-s-s-u-m {opossum}
tree {opossum-upside-down}
eyes-look-straight-out-at-me
not move
eyes-look-straight-out-at-me
attempt cover-up
fool-me
me move not same
{air-shimmer-between-us}
death wait-wait
{opossum-upside-down} nose {twitch-twitch}
{LIPS: PAH} pah

Robin | robin

strange how
they'd managed
to hide
all winter long
the two apple trees
in our backyard
never burst into
blossoms until
they revealed
their red-orange breasts
the first of spring
to come
the first of autumn
to disappear

r-o-b-i-n bird odd why
winter time {robin} disappear
all-around-gone
house back {area}
apple tree tree {one-apart-one}
spring {explode} never
r-o-b-i-n pop-up
red-orange {chest}
spring arrive pah
same-same
{them robins} disappear
autumn arrive pah
same-same

Hare | rabbit

they bounce snowshoe
ghosts of winter
sloping down
dunes cresting up
after each snowfall
past midnight
they stab
the crust of white
with pawprints
behind pellets
ellipses to
another sentence
of seasons
yet to be captured

{back-legs-stride-far-back front-legs-move-short
        bounce-bounce} snow {spread-all-over}
                wind-wind overnight
      snow {coast-up-down-all-over}
{back-legs-stride-far-back front-legs-move-short
        bounce-bounce} snow layer freeze hard
           {legs-push-hard-push-hard LIPS: EXPLOSIVE}
          morning find
p-e-l-l-e-t-s small-poop-poop
        look-like English sentence {dot dot dot}
              world out-there write-write
        book weather year-round
document-document finish not-yet

Tadpole | t-a-d-p-o-l-e

in those days
Montreal River
was rarely clear
but when it was
I could read
them darting
their eyes
tiny as periods
searching
for the perfect
sentence to end
so they could
become stories
hopping free

back-then

m-o-n-t-r-e-a-l r-i-v-e-r

filthy

but once-in-a-while clear

me spot-notice

t-a-d-p-o-l-e-s {dart-dart}

eyes same-same sentence {period point-to}

{dart-dart}

search-search

sentence perfect finish-end

become frog

{boing}

story-story pah

Flea | f-l-e-a

it all starts
with an itch
here and there
I never think
much of it
then I catch
my dog trying
to scratch again
so until then
they stay vampires
nestled in fur
claws locked in
the jugular percolating
the sweetest blood

itch-back-of-hand

{here-there-body}

think nothing

then spot-notice

d-o-g {scratch-scratch-behind-ear}

all-along moment that

itch-itch

become vampire

hide {LIPS: POW} f-u-r

{row-of-teeth TEETH-BARED

teeth-clamp-shut-on-jugular-vein

SWALLOWS}

blood sweet perfect

Butterfly | butterfly

each time
they landed
on a branch
their entire
lives in red
stained glass
peeked open
but always
closing just so
near me
my heart now
wings of autobiography
waiting to be
savored in the sun

happen tend

                                              tree {branch-sticking-out}

butterfly-float-float

                                                {talons-perch-branch}

butterfly wing

                                                    color loud red

look-like s-t-a-i-n-e-d glass

                                  {butterfly-wings opening-closing-slowly}

me want look-peek-inside curious

                                        same-same book color red

same-same heart mine what

                                                self story write

wait-wait book-open-wide-out-there

                                        sun cast-beam shine-shine

Moth | m-o-t-h

fluttering
underneath the streetlamp
with their inkwells
spilling every which way
and shaking off
the powder on their wings
they are trying
to write and rewrite
love poems
to a luminous being
already in radiance
with someone else
having promised the stars
I am smitten too

street l-a-m-p {streetlamp-head-flower-droop}
w-i-n-g-s {u-fingers-flutter-flutter
flicker-flicker-commotion right-under-lamp}
words wrong-wrong {shoot-shoot-all-over}
p-o-w-d-e-r layer {u-fingers-flutter-flutter
drift-float-all-over LIPS: EXPLODE}
words what write
poems love honor-honor who
{point-to streetlamp-head-flower-droop
person-itself shimmer-shimmer-outward}
problem fall-in-love someone other
promise stars everything theirs
me-look-up {flicker-flicker-commotion}
me-fall-in-love-upward {up-out-there}

Hawk | hawk

his wings are a warning
coasting on high
my soul a moving target
mapped by indecision
an easy prey for the taking
I pray to become
an angel right here on this altar
ledged high above
the Lake of the Clouds
crowned by a holy burst
of autumnal colors
suddenly binoculared
I am the one with talons
winged with a mission

spot-up-there h-a-w-k {fly-wings-open-coasting}
warning-warning
my soul {bull's-eye-forehead-me} person-wander
{bull's-eye-forehead-me} why ??
self doubt-doubt easy kidnap finish
pray-pray hope me-become
angel stand mountain stare-down-valley-below
L-a-k-e o-f t-h-e C-l-o-u-d-s
trees {crown-around} fall colors
shimmer-shimmer-up-outward
my eyes {binoculars-focus-focus stop-right-there}
me angel no more finish
talons ready
{wings-fly-fly} ready {spin-spin-forward}

Moose | moose

his head
crowned with
bones of war
moves slowly
to the right
then left
before he wades
past the cattails
and dragonflies
soldiering around
he catches sight
of me trying not to breathe
as he demands
hey you

head face {head-face-long LIPS: SLIGHT-PUFF}
antlers {crown-outward}
weight worth what w-a-r
himself {head-neck-forward body-forward
turn-slowly-right-left
feet-plop-right-plop-left} s-w-a-m-p
c-a-t-t-a-i-l-s {hang-low-to-left}
dragonfly-dragonfly flutter-flutter-around
moose himself move-slowly
head {turn-slowly-right}
spot-over-there me
{body-move-back} me frightened
his-eyes-wide-open-stare-at-me
{head-bob-up} what-up

Fox | fox

ears corner
the distance
measured
between prey
and predator
tail holding still
a match ready
to strike
a streak of dull
orange fire
hatcheting
through the grass
past the goldenrods
for a tasty mouse

ear-ear {point-up-triangles-head}
{head-revolve} listen-listen-sonar
distance-far
hungry
t-a-i-l {LIPS: FAT-FRONT tail-slight-arch-upright}
same-same fire-strike-match
ready
fire-streak-run
take-off {LIPS: BOOM}
dart-under
grass
g-o-l-d-e-n-r-o-d-s yellow {plant-head-droop}
dart-under catch mouse
{LICK-GULP}

Mosquito | mosquito

to them we are
walking wet
dreams of blood
pumping warm
like the sex
we ache to have
but don't get
often enough
as we want
so in the gaps
of our ache
they penetrate
our skin
those little pricks

mosquitoes obsess
us humans
mosquitoes dream
us bodies
blood full
us throb-want-throb-want
lust-lust
but enough never
more want always
us search-search
sex
mosquitoes-drill
{fuck-fuck-body-all-over}
us-annoy finish

Toad | frog

he sat staunchly
under a canopy
of dandelion leaves
in the shade
his bulbous eyes
the color of pebble
his skin
a pimpled bark
then pow
he leaped far
past my feet
how I envied
the rocket propulsion
of his legs

flower {petals-drift-away}

l-e-a-v-e-s

{canopy}

s-h-a-d-e

{eyes-oversized}

t-o-a-d

{sit-crouched-over}

s-k-i-n

{pebbled-down-face}

s-i-t

{frog-leap-far LIPS: POW}

l-e-g-s

{powerful}

e-n-v-y

{eyes-stare}

Bat | bat

they boomerang
razors so fast
they seem like
eye-blink-blink
shadows chopping
up the twilight
where the stars
are already crumbled
icing on the cake
that are morsels
of mosquitoes
fattened by blood
sugared by our days
of ice cream

{zip-zip-zip-fast LIPS: BIM} *

{eyes-blink-blink-blink-all-over LIPS: BIM}

{face-dark-slow GRIM}

{neck-chop neck-chop star-twinkle-outward-inward}

{collapse-crumble gather-up-gather-up eat-slow-eat}

us-us eat-eat ice-cream ice-cream feed-feed out-there

mosquito {body-expand-fat CHEEKS-PUFF}

{index-finger-slash-neck index-finger-slash-neck}

bat-swallow-swallow

* The use of both hands at the same time is required to perform this poem in ASL.

Bee | bee

rolling over
in a sea of clovers
looking up at
the sky whipped
by cloud streaks
I lay dreaming
of wings to fly
turning over
again I spotted
a fat bumblebee
tottering atop
a thin-necked clover
its weight pulling
us back to earth

me {legs-front-down-roll-over}
  {legs-drop} c-l-o-v-e-r-s {spill-apart}
me {on-my-back} eyes-look-up-circle
  s-k-y wind strong
c-l-o-u-d {streak-straight-across TEETH-BARED}
  eyes-look-up-circle envision-fade-away
fly-float-over-fly-float-over
  {me-legs-back-turn-front-down}
me spot-notice {LIPS: BOOM}
  b-e-e {CHEEKS-PUFF}
{curved-legs-atop-index-finger-wobbly} c-l-o-v-e-r
  b-e-e weight-heavy
our-dream fly
  us-two {crash-ground}

Strider | s-t-r-i-d-e-r

even in the hot
peat of summer
the pond is ice
enough for them
to skate across
their slenderness
a shadow floating
in the breeze
I was always afraid
of water even
with lifeguards nearby
how I wanted to skate
across the glass
of my drowning

very-hot
   not-matter
      p-o-n-d
         same-same
               freeze
                    bug
         skate-skate
      water
   me-grow-up
afraid
   drown
      me-drool
         skate-skate
              water

Sparrow | s-p-a-r-r-o-w

after the boys once again
mocked my speech
I glanced up
at the power line
a string of black pearls
bobbing slightly
from their wings
a-twitter with shrugs
as they got on and off
as if it were a train car
how I longed to shrink
my gangly body down
into the tiniest wings
and disappear

again-again BIG-SIGH

them boys mock-me speech MOCK-OVERENUNCIATE

me-look-up LIPS: OPEN-IN-WONDER

electricity line-drop-rise-line LIPS: CLOSED-OOO

birds same p-e-a-r-l necklace black LIPS: BLIP-BLIP

{tiny-flutters-line-drop-rise} LIPS: BLIP-BLIP

{folded-wings-adjust-adjust} DISCOMFORT

{folded-wings-adjust-finish} CONTENTED

electricity line {bird-hop-on take-off} LIPS: PUM-PUM

same-same train {people-get-on get-off} SERIOUS

me-look-up electricity line SMALL-SIGH

me-want my-body {shrink-down tiny box} LIPS: THIN

wings {shrink-down-tiny} fly-small AFRAID

flap-hard {large-up-close-shrink-distance} SMILE

Chipmunk | c-h-i-p-m-u-n-k

one bit me
when I was five
at Bay Cliff Health Camp
I have no recollection
of how I extended
my finger
even now
years later
their brown eyes
still peer at me
from the side
asking if that family story
about me
was indeed true

me age five
happen
B-a-y C-l-i-f-f Health Camp
c-h-i-p-m-u-n-k {bite-my-finger}
happen how
{point-to-finger}
{move-finger-to-chipmunk}
not remember
years later
still {them} eyes brown
{them-look-at-me-from-the-side}
ask-ask each-other
family story relate-to me
true-biz happen ??

Leech | l-e-e-c-h

they found our legs
easily if we stood
too long in the warmth
of Montreal River
around our shoulders
we'd never feel them
suckling like plastic
wrap around our thighs
when we left the water
to partake in hot dogs
and chips we found
those sludgy commas
how we screamed
and scraped them off

us   kids   stand-stand   water   m-o-n-t-r-e-a-l   r-i-v-e-r

long time warm perfect water {float-float-around-shoulders}

not feel l-e-e-c-h {down-water} stick-to {FIRM-KISS} l-e-g-s

not   feel   {stick-to-all-over}   water   same-same

p-l-a-s-t-i-c   w-r-a-p   water   finish

us hungry go table {over-there} hot-dogs potato c-h-i-p-s

{walk-out}   water   look-down   black   {bumps-down-skin}

scream-scream {push-off-skin} scream {push-off-skin DISGUST}

Otter | o-t-t-e-r

in a documentary
they dove in
into the burble
of river, braiding
around each other
their combed fur
shining in the sun
their eyes twinkling
watching them
I wished my siblings
had been more like them
always pulling me in
to cavort with them

me watch-watch d-o-c-u-m-e-n-t-a-r-y
{creature-wriggle creature-wriggle}
water {cascade-left-right-down}
{creature-dive-down creature-rise-up
around-each-other
fur-lining-arms-chest} wet
sun {on-me}
shine-shine
eyes
shine-shine
me wish brother-sister
same-{otters}
come-on-come-on
play-play

Goose | goose

come september
the sky
jolted in blue
slashed
with
an arrowhead
drawing, fluttering,
in slow motion
a v of wings
cascading higher
while I long
to feel such wind on my face
but my feet
aren't feathered

september *
sky
blue-blue
up-there
wings
stretched
tips-slight-flutter
another tips-slight-flutter up
another tips-slight-flutter up
bounce-bounce-up
triangle {look-up-nod}
wind-rush-past-my-face {nod
LIPS: SIGH} wings-out-fly-drop-like-stone
swing-to-feet-drop-stuck

* This poem uses flat handshapes only.

Lynx | l-y-n-x

the earth
a frozen heart
is covered
with layers
of snow
I know
summer must
exist
inside but
I am stranded
outside with
my thick paws
hunting for
prey of affection

ball-of-earth

ball-of-heart-on-chest

{cover-ball-of-heart}

snow-fall

{ball-of-heart} layer {ball-of-heart}

inside {ball-of-heart}

warm

have

must

but me-stuck

{huge-dome-out-there}

me-lonely

search-search

hug-hug warmth

Snake | snake

the first time
I held one
in my own hands
it wriggled
from struggle
its skin uncoiling
trying to write
on the papyrus
of my hands
my destiny
the future
of the boy
I hadn't yet molted
to become a man

[*index finger*]   first
time
{snake}

[*two hands*]   {open-hands}
{wriggle-across}
{struggle-struggle}

[*two hands*]   write-write
hand-hand
paper-paper

{pause}

[*flat hand*]   future
my-self
man

Hummingbird | hummingbird

my heart beats
really lightning
when I spot
the glorious flower
of you basking
again in the sun
I feel as if I can fly
I feel already high
your tongue hangs
awaiting mine
together we will
cream dreams
of spring
nectar come fill me

{index finger-thumb open-close-quickly-over-heart}
lightning {hand-open-there LIPS: BOOM}

{hands-down-up-you} flower {petals-open you}
sun {you} shimmer-shine shimmer-shine

me-feel fly-fly can
me-feel mind-high

{you your-tongue-wrap-around-mine
bodies-together explode LIPS: PUFF}

spring finish
{eat-slurp eat-slurp}

Woodpecker | woodpecker

the holes
left behind
in the bark
are messages
once tap-
drummed
out in
telegrams
echoing
across the web
of forests
now forlorn
with songs
for the lovelorn

tree

{dot}

{dot-down}

{dot-down}

inform-inform

{middle-finger-stuck-out-heart-throb}

inform-inform

{tweet-off-index-finger-tweet-off-index-finger}

woods-all-around

hear what

sing-sing

{flat-rhythm-over-heart}

one-lonely

{one-one} stand-far-apart

Bear | bear

cluttered among artifacts
of the Historical Society Museum
he loomed tall
a shadow, his fur
stiff and lined
with pearls of dust
his angled paws
big as plates
his claws
commas of danger
staring above me to the window
his eyes mirrored mine
those were the days
when I wished I were dead

history society museum small but all-over shelf-shelf

table-table   a-r-t-i-f-a-c-t-s   different-different

but   one   me-jaw-drop   b-e-a-r   tall   big   f-u-r   black

thin-layer   arm   d-u-s-t   stand   {arms-slightly-outreached-

paws-ready-to-pounce}   c-l-a-w-s   long   danger-danger   whew

but   stand-stand   eyes   {arms-slightly-outreached-paws-ready-

to-pounce}   stare   {eyes-sail-over-my-head-look}   window

my   eyes   same-him   back-then   me-obsess   me-wish   dead

Squirrel | squirrel

amidst the birches
and tall grasses
its tips waving in the wind
I found one
sprawled dead
its hide punctured
by beak
its stiff tail
wisps flapping
in the wind
as if never had
a chance to say
goodbye
to these trees

tree b-i-r-c-h trees-in-a-half-circle
grass {shimmer-grow-tall
grass-leaves-undulate-wind-undulate}
me-spot-down-there {LIPS: BOOM}
squirrel {legs-sprawl-twist TONGUE-SIDEWAYS
side-of-chest scar-down LIPS: FIRM-PUFF}
bird {scar-down} that
legs-sprawl-twist} wind-wind
t-a-i-l {tail-flap-bye-flap-bye}
same-same
try-here try-there
waving-goodbye-around-in-a-half-circle
can't .

Crow | c-r-o-w

they blacken the skies
with their paintbrushes
when they alight on trees
in the dim of winter
they are the only color
that prods me forward
when I ache for the sky
canvas to rip apart in blue
letting the palette of sun
melting the primed snow
whenever I step out
they critique me cawing
observations awaiting
the masterpiece of my death

winter gray {across-sky-up-there DEPRESSED}
c-r-o-w {hands-up-apart-shimmer-float-downward}
trees-half-line {trees-line-up} street-opposite home
{shimmer-float-downward} tree {perch-branch}
me look-across {crows-in-trees FEAR}
color black {theirs-across bother-bother-me} why
s-k-y me-hunger-lust-hunger-lust {hands-tear-apart-sky}
gray {across-sky no-more} b-l-u-e {across-sky} pah
sun {throw-light} color-color loud {LIPS: BOOM}
snow {fall-on-everything} melt
still me out move-about-outside
{point-crows-trees} birds observe-me wait-wait
criticize-criticize-me {mouths-talk-talk gossip-gossip}
me die perfect

Porcupine | porcupine

hiding up in the trees
as if detached from
my name-stoned body
I see them boys
guffawing at me
my body is
a cluster of quills
my heart is
an inkwell of bile
how I must keep
hunting for a safe
place to write
in order to survive

hearing school boys {them}
pick-on-me-pick-on-me
me-try defend-myself
label-label-label-hand-forearm
look-at-me laugh-laugh-laugh
permit-me feel pain-hurt refuse
instead my-body soul let-go-each-other
me-hide trees-half-circle {up-there}
my-body {four-fingers-crown-around-finger}
my-heart anger word-word-word-list overflow
{them-boys} replace-replace-replace-across
search-search home feel safe
{four-fingers-crown-around-finger pluck-quill}
i-n-k {quill-dip} write-on-label-label-hand-forearm
{raise-labeled-forearm-up-to-power-fist}

Turtle | turtle

may the alkalinity
of my anger
righteously mine
filter right out
the house of me
may the weight
of my gravel tears
slide off the roof
of my bruises
so I may sail
down the river
up Lake Superior
where I'll never
need a house like that

[*flat hands*]

{LIPS: GIBBERISH stumble-interact CONFUSED}

anger

simmer-simmer

my-body

house

filter-filter {DISGUST}

clean-out

[*"A" handshape*]

suffer

tears-suffer-out-of-eyes

{fists-beat-my-body}

[*flat hands*]

sail-gently-side-to-side-river

{boat-opens-up-wide-water}

[*"A" handshape | flat hands*]

my-self house hide-turtle no-more

Bobcat | b-o-b-c-a-t

just past the twilight
before my planned suicide
I dreamed they'd
be so hungry that
they'd slip through
my bedroom window
and pounce on me
without a sound
slashing my throat
so I would never speak
my terrible ache to die
they'd leave me alive
so I could transmogrify
into a stronger cat

one night
many-thoughts-flicker-in-head {SERIOUS}
me-want die
envision b-o-b-c-a-t-s what

{gallop-gallop head-first-ram LIPS: BAM}
bedroom window {explode-shatter
four-paws-land-leap-off land-on-me
paw-claws-slash-my-throat TEETH-BARED}
speak again can't
me-want-want die stop
{them-gallop-pounce-out} window
me left alive

time progress
become c-a-t strong future

Cardinal | c-a-r-d-i-n-a-l

in the grayest of days
I thought of love
bled out of my marrow
wanting the ice kiss
of death to overtake me
I sought a clearing
of birches whose peelings
spoke a whole new language
impossible to decipher
explaining why I had to die
a cardinal flew suddenly
out of a snow-laced evergreen
its redness startled my heart
until I melted into spring

lonely days *
me think {SAD}
{draw-heart-over-heart-on-chest}

{blood-extract-from-forearm-vein} **
stand-fall-back
throat-stuck {head-drop-to-the-side eyes-closed
TONGUE-SLIGHTLY-OUT}

me-arrive trees-in-a-half-circle ***
{bark-wrap-wrap-around-tree peel-back
open-up-pull-apart-scroll flat-hand-up-read-down
shake-head-no NOT-UNDERSTAND}

surprise red bird {beak-open-shut-fly-outward ****
draw-heart-over-heart-on-chest LIPS: EXPECTANT}

{hands-crossed-over-heart SMILE-CONTENTED}

---

   * Only index fingers are used in the first stanza.

  ** Only the "2" handshape is used in the second stanza.

 *** Only flat hands are used in the third and last stanzas.

**** Only the "G" handshape is used in the fourth stanza.

Skunk | skunk

unseen they waddled
among the grasses
across the street
their white stripes
a warning flash
some nights
their smell of danger
swung low
like fog packed down
pulling me to the ground
as if hands
vised around my neck
marking my nose
forevermore

me-see skunk never
{tail-waddle-fist} grass overlook
trees opposite-street mom house
white {point-to-head-down-back}
warn {headlights-flash-flash}
once-while night
smell strong stink
spread-out
heavy same-same f-o-g
smell {pull-me-down}
similar {hands-choke-my-neck}
skunk {standing-upside-down}
stink {spray-throw-at-me}
my-nose dead finish

Cow | cow

her eyes
almost black
blinked slowly
at me
as we stood
facing each other
in a 4-H barn
as the aura of hay
and manure
wafted around us
I wondered
how I'd smelled to her
a human boy with milk

eyes

dark

blink

stare-me

us-stand-facing-each-other

b-a-r-n

smell

h-a-y

poop

waft-around-us

me-wonder

herself

smell

milk

inside

me

can

??

Wolf | wolf

having howled
among evergreens
they sniff
the moon
on high
a song
that never
answers back
the hills
are marrowed
with ghost
dogs buried
deep inside
their bones

howl finish *

sniff-sniff

{hands-offer-up-to-moon}

song {up-there}

arrive-down here {shake-head-no}

hills-slope-up-down-up-down

bury bury bury

bones-crossing-chest

* Only flat hands are used for the entire poem except for the last line.

Duck | duck

I never knew
his name
but he was quite
a sight so beautiful
his hair
a slick dark green
his collar
a white ring
his suit jacket
buffed in earth tones
the boy I loved
from afar
was a swan

boy me-fall-in-love
name his not-know
but wow
himself beautiful
him-comb-hair {SMUG}
dark green shine
{collar-ring-around-the-neck}
white {neck-shine}
jacket {suit-tie}
brown black gray proper colors
boy me-fall-in-love
distant
himself
s-w-a-n shimmer

Marten | marten

snaking underneath
some knitted pines
like the intrepid explorer
I was I saw
a rustle on branch
a blip of rust
maybe a little white
the pines swallowed
the shadow of no name
what was that I wondered
what if I had no name
what if I was indeed
a wild animal nobody wanted
to acknowledge

tree-tree p-i-n-e {stand-scrunged-together}
me {try-weave-under}
big-ego dart-under-there can chin-pow {DARE}
me-spot-over-there
tree {many-branch-stick-out}
{move-into-tree LIPS: BLIP}
color r-u-s-t
possible white
s-h-a-d-o-w {movement-circle-disappear LIPS: BLIP
glance-there scan-watch} that what {QUESTION}
me-wonder i-f me-same-same animal w-i-l-d
name none recognize none
hearing-people
prefer overlook-me

Tick | t-i-c-k

never had to think
about those things
when I scampered
into the woods
across the street
where deer hid
now I hear stories
from friends
now I must check
the crannies
of my socks
and my body
how I must
delouse my memories

back-then
think danger-danger
never
trees-in-a-half-circle
opposite-street
deer hide where
over-there
now friends
warn-warn-me
walk trees-in-a-half-circle finish
now investigate must what t-i-c-k-s
look-down-legs socks {pull-apart}
observe-observe-my-body mirror
memories infection clean-clean

Rat | rat

their tails
serpent
between
the walls
their feet
a hush
whiskers
scraping
for crumbs
off plates
unwiped
next up
dessert
poison

w-a-l-l-s

{two-walls-facing-each-other-closely-together-ahead}

rat t-a-i-l

{slither-against-wall

their-feet-scurry finger-to-the-lips SHHH}

plate dirty c-r-u-m-b-s

{snout-eat-eat whiskers-brush-brush}

next dessert what

medicine poison

Weasel | w-e-a-s-e-l

they glee
like needles
threading
the fabric
of forest
rising high
above river
their movements
stitching together
a chaotic tapestry
until they loom
white-bellied
paint streaks
into the dark

[*index fingers*]	{criss-cross-all-over-each-other}
	same-same
	{needle-down-up-around-edge}
[*flat hands*]	stage-curtain
	curtain-rises
	tree-tree-tree
	reveal-out-there
	{water-cascade-down-river
[*index fingers* |	criss-cross-all-over-each-other}
flat hands]	out-there mass-confusion
	{criss-cross-all-over-each-other}
	darken-slowly
	but eye-spot {LIPS: BOOM}
	white zig-zag-lightning

Cougar | c-o-u-g-a-r

allegedly still a few
lurk like specters
sleeping behind logs
always listening
for the sound of me
among the goldenrods
and the tall grasses
dancing to distract
me wondering maybe
bigfoot may not live
around these parts
but they are biding
their scheduled time
to whisper again

rumor-rumor   few   still   hide   here   there   sleep   where

tree-fallen   behind   listen-rotate-listen-rotate

me   dart-among   g-o-l-d-e-n-r-o-d-s   grass   {grow-

tall   wind-grass-undulate}   overlook-overlook

me-look-away   wonder-wonder   B-i-g-f-o-o-t

somewhere-over-there   probably   not   but

c-o-u-g-a-r-s   hide   wait-wait   time

spread-all-out   {LIPS: BOOM}   pah

Grasshopper | grasshopper

they waited
tense as
clothespins
clinging
to the wire
then a bomb
of movement
in the distance
they moved
a fingersnap
of wind
across the grass
leaves
mushrooming

{paws-curved-shoulders-crouched STARE} *

outside clothes line {clothespin-clothespin-finger}

{paws-curved-shoulders-crouched STARE}

distance far {wind-startle-trees}

{paws-curved-shoulders-crouched STARE}

{fingersnaps LIPS: BOOM}

{paws-drop-fists-push-down-leap-paws-explode
grasshoppers-leap-spread-outward-bounce} **

* In the first, third, and fifth stanzas, there should be no motion for a moment.
** This stanza should be done in slow-motion.

Cockroach | cockroach

apparently they could survive
even a nuclear apocalypse
their armored backs
mirroring the flashpoint
highlighting the greed
that's strip-mined so much
this rare earth that we walk on
under the ghost clouds
sifting the flour of radiation
into the passages of memory
circulating inside our bodies
until we are shell-shocked
cancered into extinction
may they do better than us

seems *

n-u-c-l-e-a-r {explosion-destruction} survive can

{cockroach-back-waddle-forearm}

reflect shine dollar-signs-eyes

mirror

out-there {scratch-scratch-destroy DETERMINED}

{curved-hands-mound}

{cloud-swirl-shimmer-spread-down} r-a-d-i-a-t-i-o-n

{fall-down-slowly drift-toward-chest land-sharp}

remember-remember {hands-shimmer-circles-body}

{full-mind-shock}

c-a-n-c-e-r destroy all-us future

{cockroach-back-waddle-forearm} stubborn

* Starting with this line (and every other line),
  use only the curved-open handshape.

Firefly | f-i-r-e-f-l-y

the fall of dusk
the flutter of bats
the keening of owls
the ponder of mice
the silhouette of trees
the stiffness of leaves
doubling up against
the buffeting of autumn
on this lonely street
windows eyelidded shut
to hide the REM of TVs
the firefly is a lighthouse
blinking for hope
in this small world

darkness-close-slowly
bat {flutter-above}
{owl-eyes-focusing-slowly-rotate-back-and-forth}
mice {eyes-slowly-rotate-back-and-forth}
tree {shimmer-backward} s-h-a-d-o-w
{tree-crown} l-e-a-v-e-s {leaf-hand}
wind-wind {leaf-grip-hard FIRM}
autumn soon
out-there street lonely-lonely
house-house window {shade-pull-down}
t-v color-color {tiny-eye-blinks}
world chaos but
f-i-r-e-f-l-y light {big-blink-big-blink-all-over}
hope still {look-up} out-there

II.

Wild Animals, Again

Animals don't speak, don't they?

How foolish of us to assume
how superior we are to them animals:

how else to explain crows
relaying to their kind
which of us humans are good:

somehow they transmit
images of their allies
to their friends who in turn
transmit to their own friends:

can telepathy
of a very different language
exist between animals?

*

animals out-there speak not right ??

us ego-big-head assume
them-out-there beneath-us

strange c-r-o-w-s seem chin-pow
person self good bird look mind snapshot
telepathy-telepathy-all-over point person trust

seem c-r-o-w-s out-there
information share telepathy
spread all-across a-l-l-round recognize person trust

animals out-there
telepathy have
meaning language different have ??

Whose language matters
more in the wilderness
forested with our hands,
starved and skeletony
from no water of information
nor the chlorophyll of affection,
now a landscape of barren
trees shorn of leaves
while the rest of our bodies
rot and weep
among the mycologia
swelling with spore
underground, waiting
for the right moment
to unleash and shine?

*

language human which
important pah
out-there w-i-l-d
hands ours
starve-starve bone-bone
information world none
affection cherish none
out-there now
trees body-naked winter
bodies ours
fall-apart weep-weep-fall-down
out-there mushrooms
{cheeks-expand} spread-across
wait-wait time right
{mouth-expel-air} grow-apart shine

What is "wild" out there:

no paths easy enough
for us, no trees tall
enough to keep us cool,
no burbles of creek
to catch the bouncing sun:

whose idea of beauty is
this:

a blanket of perfect-
ly watered grass
so verdant, trimmed
of weeds pushing
through sidewalk
cracks, a jolt:

or a shag carpet of
native grasses topped
with flowers listening
to no one but the earth,
waving with the breeze:

" " w-i-l-d {point-to} mean what

wander-among easy not
trees above-us cool not
water shimmer-shimmer-down not

beauty define decide who ??

compare here-there

{here}
grass green-green wow
water perfect
mow-mow all-over
w-e-e-d-s none
w-e-e-d-s pop-up s-i-d-e-w-a-l-k none
eye-spot finish

{there}
grass {grow-grow-fire-all-over}
flowers ignore world
flowers heart-feel earth-ball
{body-sway-sway}

yet beavers engineer
precious cradles
of rainwater
from the latticework
of sapling-woven
dams in the swamp:

suddenly among
the ugliest patches
(according to
our misformed eyes),
creatures congregate
to partake in
the sweetest water:

the river mouths
sing louder,
a choir that has
nothing to do with us
humans:

beavers chin-pow
water control-manage
rain-rain water
d-a-m set-up-here-there-over-there
s-w-a-m-p

seem out-there
{eyes-scan-across-landscape}
u-g-l-y whew
but strange
animals different-different
gather-together
water clean-clean wow
{trickle-trickle-down-throat}

river loud-boom
sing
us humans {ears-flip-back-deaf}

animals must wonder
why we expend so much
energy to protect us
from ourselves:

when we lose power,
pixels are wind,
a song that we'd forgotten
how to sing
the first moment
we stopped talking
to each other
in real time:

animals will outlive
us when we find ourselves
unable to speak
the language of connection.

animals watch-watch-us
wonder-wonder why
us humans scared
animals {inside-chest} have

electricity gone
smartphones soon nothing
time long-ago
us humans wind study-study understand-clearly
but forgot minute focus each-other
ignore wind

animals overtake ball-earth reign will
why
us humans connect deep can't
language fail

Acknowledgements

Some poems in English were published with ASL gloss; some, not:

Clementine Unbound: "Moose."
FENCE: "Duck."
Ginosko Literary Journal: "Skunk."
Hotel: "Flea."
Laurel Review: "Chipmunk" and "Weasel."
Midway Journal: "Hummingbird."
Midwest Review: "Cow" and "Squirrel."
Poem-a-Day: "Otters."
Poet Lore: "Deer," "Hare," and "Turtle."
River Mouth Review: "Bee."
Salamander: "Bat."

U.P. Reader: Bringing Upper Michigan Literature to the World (Volume 6) (Mikel Classen and Deborah K. Frontiera, eds.; Modern History Press): "Woodpecker."

The poem "Grasshoppers" was used as part of the Red Wing Arts 21st Annual Poet Artist Collaboration (April 14–May 15, 2022).

The poem "Cow" was nominated for a Pushcart Prize.

In Gratitude

The author is most grateful to Patrick Davis and
Peter Campion for believing in this unusual book, and
to Cory Firestine for facilitating the process of bringing
Animals Out-There W-i-l-d to your hands.

He is equally indebted to Eric Thomas Norris and Tom Steele
for their enduring faith in my work. Special thanks go to
Ching-In Chen, Jonathan Johnson, Ellen Lord, and Eric Thomas
Norris for their kind words about this book.

David Cummer (1956 — 2022) and I used to text each other
occasionally in ASL gloss. He'd have been delighted and proud
that such a book as this now exists. May his memory continue
to be a blessing.

About the Author

Raymond Luczak lost most of his hearing at the age of eight months due to double pneumonia and a high fever, but this was not detected until he was two-and-a-half years old. After all, he was just number seven in a hearing family of nine children growing up in Ironwood, a small mining town in Michigan's Upper Peninsula (U.P.). Forbidden to sign, he was outfitted with a rechargeable hearing aid and started on speech therapy immediately. At 14 years old, he demanded to learn how to sign. Four years later, he ended up at Gallaudet University, where he learned American Sign Language (ASL).

Luczak is the author and editor of over 30 books, including the poetry collections *Chlorophyll*, *Lunafly*, and *Far from Atlantis; once upon a twin* was selected as a Top Ten U.P. Notable Book of the Year for 2021. His prose titles include *A Quiet Foghorn: More Notes from a Deaf Gay Life*, *From Heart into Art: Interviews with Deaf and Hard of Hearing Artists and Their Allies*, and the award-winning Deaf gay novel *Men with Their Hands*. His most recent anthologies as editor are *Yooper Poetry: On Experiencing Michigan's Upper Peninsula* and *Oh Yeah: A Bear Poetry Anthology*. His work has appeared in *Poetry*, *Prairie Schooner*, and elsewhere. A proud Yooper native and an inaugural Zoeglossia Poetry Fellow, he lives in Minneapolis, Minnesota.

About the Type and Paper

Designed by Malou Verlomme of the Monotype Studio, Macklin is an elegant, high-contrast typeface. It has been designed purposely for more emotional appeal.

The concept for Macklin began with research on historical material from Britain and Europe dating to the beginning of the 19th century, specifically the work of Vincent Figgins. Verlomme pays respect to Figgins's work with Macklin, but pushes the family to a more contemporary place.

This book is printed on natural Rolland Enviro Book stock. The paper is 100 percent post-consumer sustainable fiber content and is FSC-certified.

Animals Out-There W-i-l-d was designed by Eleanor Safe and Joseph Floresca.

Unbound Edition Press champions honest, original voices. Committed to the power of writers who explore and illuminate the contemporary human condition, we publish collections of poetry, short fiction, and essays. Our publisher and editorial team aim to identify, develop, and defend authors who create thoughtfully challenging work which may not find a home with mainstream publishers. We are guided by a mission to respect and elevate emerging, under-appreciated, and marginalized authors, with a strong commitment to advancing LGBTQ+ and BIPOC voices. We are honored to make meaningful contributions to the literary arts by publishing their work.

unboundedition.com